CW01477024

THE ROAD TAKEN

THE ROAD TAKEN

Patrick Howse

with paintings by
Inge Schlaile

HAYLOFT

First published in Great Britain 2020 by Hayloft Publishing Ltd.

© Patrick Howse, 2020
Images © Inge Schlaile, 2020

The right of Patrick Howse to be identified as the Author of this Work
has been asserted by him in accordance with the Copyright, Designs
and Patents Act 1988

All rights reserved. Apart from any use permitted under UK copyright
law no part of this publication may be reproduced, stored in a retrieval
system, or transmitted, in any form or by any means without the prior
written permission of the publisher, nor be otherwise circulated in any
form of binding or cover other than that in which it is published and
without a similar condition being imposed on the subsequent purchaser.

A CIP catalogue record for this book is available from the British Library

ISBN 978-1-910237-42-7

Designed, printed and bound in the EU

Hayloft policy is to use papers that are natural, renewable and
recyclable products and made from wood grown in sustainable forests.
The logging and manufacturing processes are expected to conform to
the environmental regulations of the country of origin.

Climate neutral
Print product
ClimatePartner.com/12667-1910-1001

This book was printed with the offset of carbon emissions and
support for Forest Protection in Pará, Brazil.

Hayloft Publishing Ltd,
a company registered in England number 4802586
2 Staveley Mill Yard, Staveley, Kendal, LA8 9LR (registered office)
L'Ancien Presbytère, 21460 Corsaint, France (editorial office)

Email: books@hayloft.eu
Tel: +44 (0)7971 352473
www.hayloft.eu

To Ellie, Joe and Clara
and
To Inge
Who brought light
To the darkness
With love.

Also by Patick Howse

Shadow Cast by Mountains (2017)

Contents

Introduction

The poems in this book were written as I made the transition from living and working in England, to starting a new life in Germany.

They are a response (but not an answer) to works by Robert Frost and Edward Thomas, both of whom I admire. Frost chose his path in the woods, though he seems to have more interest in the one he spurned, and Thomas' poems all glow with the background radiation of the choice he had to make – whether or not to go to war a century ago.

I have chosen my road, and it is one that I tread hand-in-hand with Inge Schlaile ('Schlinge').

Her paintings in this book derive from the same starting point as my poems, but they stand and speak for themselves – they are not intended as illustrations of my work.

Britain's chosen road – the vote to leave the European Union – was the catalyst for our decision to leave the UK. I've been appalled by the re-emergence of intolerance, racism and fascism in English society, and in retrospect I can see that I never felt that I fully belonged. I have been an outsider in the northern community where I grew up, in Kent where I was living when the Brexit vote was taken, and in London, that magnificent world-city where I lived and worked for twenty years.

Now I live in Germany, and I can 'not belong' here comfortably, because that lack of belonging is no surprise or challenge to anybody. I'm European, and for as long as I can I shall continue making the case for a Europe that is open, tolerant, and free.

With regard to the poems themselves, I'm concerned with the environment, the rise of the far right, mental health, love, life and death. They are divided into three parts – No Peace deals broadly with my agonising decision to leave England (probably for good); A Wound Acknowledged can be seen as explorations of new landscapes (in several different senses); and To The One is concerned with the struggles ahead.

Ultimately I believe what's important is to say the things that need to be said – and to do so in my own voice.

Patrick Howse
Munich, Christmas, 2019

PART ONE

NO PEACE

The Road Taken

Hand in hand we walk
Where tumbled rocks
Meet Rhine-sifted silt
Generously dumped
To shore-up England.

I lead a child
Beneath chalk cliffs
To be told she's taking
The path with her,
To find the way.

Crying gulls drive back
The fleeing tide
In complicated pulses
As the wind whispers sadly,
'You'll find no peace here'.

To Robert Frost and Edward Thomas

The Train To London Bridge

Smug, embittered Kent
Yields slowly to the city;
A last tunnel ends with steep
Embankments scruffily clothed

In brambles and willow-herb,
Made suddenly beautiful
By the co-incidence
Of our passing and sunshine.

We crawl towards Deptford,
(Where Marlowe died and my
Mother was born) through
Scrubby buddleia poking

Stubbornly from stone:
White butterflies feed
On spiky purple flowers
That stab as we pass.

The Train to Tunbridge Wells

Packed with the sifted
plankton of the City
a creaking old carriage
sings to whales,

Squeaking as it swims
 against contrary tides
(and signals) to creep
 into submerging darkness,

Slowly yet gracelessly
sliding away from lights
on high towers to a final
beaching in the suburbs.

Dawn

Gold slowly seeps
Into the forest;

Sun blesses trees
Waiting for winter.

9th November 2016

Shepherd's Warning

Scots pines,
growing a long century,
now stand defined by

layered
mists of blood and purple
rising from England.

17th January 2017

Waiting in a Wood

Beneath the dark shade
Cast by pine and beech
A rotting tree-trunk lies
Black at heart.

It draws me in,
Dragging me through
An ancient labyrinth
Too dense for light.

Around me holly,
Gorse and brambles
Hedge the space,
And a thousand birds sing.

England

The forest, gold brown,
dripping blood,
crowds
a naked beech.

It stood
a hundred years
before deer
browsed
bark in a ring.

Embedded
roots dissolve
in wet leaf
nourished
earth.

The branches
claw at
a callous
boiling
winter sky.

Pippingford Park

Mists thread through
Trees standing stark
Before veils of scarlet and gold;

A black deer stumbles
To disappear in tangled
Dead-brown bracken,

And slowly, leaf
By falling leaf,
The forest changes.

To Charles Jacques

Beeches

I would lie
Beneath the hedge
That surrounded

My childhood
For long summers
Without school,

Learning how brown
Leaves enrich
A fruitcake soil

Layered with
The bones
Of my fathers.

Now green leaves
Flinch as rain falls
To earth a continent deep.

Dinckley

It was an adventure
To trek through
Plumped green fields
Down to a river

Running shallow over stones
To collect cold
In deep still pools
Fit, we thought, for bears.

Now I know just how tame
These wilds are
And how close to
The town I escaped,

The small, resentful town
That blithely
Denies its rivers
Flow into a sea.

Leaving England

Purple shadow pools
beneath a burning flood
of golden light.

The chalk folds
gently into hills
formed from the crushed

Bones of my ancestors,
and the winter sun
sinks beyond the shore.

The Stain of the Years

I have looked at last
into the face of my brother,

unknown to me and strange,
the baby my mother yearned for

me to save, an old man
with a pale face, laid out

on lush green grass
with daisies at his feet.

Growing Up

A sea of sheep-
Cropped moors
Fades away in waves;

The sharp red sun
Sinks beyond
The ridge through mist

Into a darkness
That silences
Lamenting lapwings.

A lone thorn tree,
Leafless, stark,
Stretches its shadow

Towards a heart
Painfully gripped
By desperate ecstasy.

Photograph © Martin Roberts.

Beyond is the Sea

The stone washed flags
End where the beach
Wipes its feet;

The ebbing light
Kisses the ruffled water,
And a barred horizon

Slices the world
Into three strips.
Here, in shadow,

I stand wrapped
In the false dark
Warmth of hesitation.

For Martin John Roberts

The Seagulls' Mourning Cries

A shortcut to the beach
Avoids the war memorial,
But the Portland stone
Can be glimpsed
Through the trees.

A bare-breasted man
Chases a toddler
Across the sand
While she pursues
Her stumbling legs;

They both laugh,
Knowing this is to be
The best thing
In the whole world;
And it's over in a blink.

Passchendaele Centenary,
31st July '17

Missing Her Birthday

Our layered arms
Form the tricolour
Of our independence

In the cuddle after
The little girl's bleary
Stumble to our bed.

I'm dragged away
Through August
Drizzle to a train

While they play
In sunshine as
Intense as imagination

Through sea and sandy
Laughter as distant
As the cries of the gulls.

Writing on the Beach

I form neat words
in the sand
with a stick.

Beneath swift clouds
the tide turns
and brings

The cleansing sea
to wipe away
every trace.

Reading Poems by the Sea

Gulls' wings flashing
Brilliant for an instant
In a cold clear sky.

They live only
When we sing their song
And set them free.

Echoes

The sunset makes
The dust of June
Warm and glorious.

A small boy screams,
Closely watching
His head-scarfed mother;

She sheds
Silent tears
While he joyfully

Twists the embedded
Knife deeper
Into the wound,

And the departing god
Conjures a sudden frost-mist
Dusk of mid-winter.

Parting

On my
last night
I tell her
to be good.

I will,
she says,
I will be
tomorrow.

A Glimpse

Clouds shade away
To horizons that echo
Waves of dream-blue woods.

Through soft fields
And light drizzle
A horse is running,

Its head defined
Pale by chestnut flanks,
Letting me see

Beneath, to history,
To bare bones,
Bared teeth, and a horror

Stare of recognition:
We do to them
What we do to us.

The receding greys
Drag me towards
An England lost.

Leaf Ghost

On the side of this road
I trod this leaf into the slab
To rot and stain the pavement.
It left a skeletal imprint,

A faint delicate outline
Of the leaf's essence;
A phantom of the past summer,
A suggestion of its past life.

Freesias By Her Bed

Her life collapsed
To a last exquisite
Expansion of lungs

Drawing in a scent:
It led her through
The garden paths

Of youth and love
She would never
Tread again.

I might perhaps
Have dreamt her
Flower-perfumed sigh.

for Margaret Howse
1925-2004

Spring Shower

Sun-dried earth accepts
The offered rain:
A gentleness soaks

And swells the English soil
Right up to the rampant
Fresh green nettles

Poking through the wall's base.
Busy creatures crawl
From intricate crevices

While the song birds
Ignore all attempts
To fence them out.

Wörthsee

Ripples of the sun
Flare in the water
Defining the pine-blue
Trees with shadow.

Bobbing heads mark
Complex channels,
Otter-wake trailing
On the edge of a shout.

Beyond a path
of small sharp stones
A wet man lies
Separated, observing:

Every shape of human body
Drapes unselfconsciously;
A breeze blows boats
Into life, bulging

Their sails pleasantly
Bikini-round and full;
No one here
Is waiting to die.

Summer Sunset

A drop of molten gold
Slowly
Falls from slate-grey cloud

Into a band of fire
Searing
The sharp horizon.

The old god is given
His due –
A span of glory –

Before the falling dark
Swallows
Him in purple night.

Flying from Munich (Global Warming)

A sun-set
in silver,
burnished copper
and gold,
worthy of
a Viking hoard.

Cloud
blankets Europe,
a ghost of the ice
that carved
the horizon's
snowed-in mountains:

Tundra,
a wilderness
beneath the dome
of the sky,
shading deep blue
from the rim's fire.

                    To Mahalah
                    (who lent me her pen)

Autumn Music

A sky washed clean
By wind from the mountains
Shivers branches to crackle gold In the
sunlight.
A leaf, fluttering free,
Taps twice at the window,
An invitation from a butterfly
Of its season.

Observation of the Excluded Child

Behind the large glass doors
a teenaged girl lies on the floor,
kicking her feet and reading
an outspread paper.

She tears off a narrow strip
and chews it meditatively,
thinking of Bobby Kennedy.

The room is filled with
a gramophone: I'm a Believer.
"Why?", I ask, fifty years later.

Outside the sun dances on a pond,
then plays with butterflies,
and is split into tiny rainbows
in the dew-soaked lavender.

Munich: A Biergarten in October

Horse chestnuts distil
Gold from the sun
In the glory
Of their decay.
Beneath the wheeling
Sky the ancient
Alchemy still
Works its magic;
And in silhouette
A stark, dark tree
Stands with treasure
Around its feet.

Autumn

A pale low sun
chases me
through bare trees;

A train drags
us away from
the summer.

Neighbours

Red squirrels run
The length of the street
Without touching the ground,

And above the crow-
Topped trees a building
Shines in sunset gold.

Reflected hot windows
Screen the glinting people
Living part-lives exposed:

I know the colour
Of their underwear
But their voices are strangers.

I stand mute in my
Still purple shadow's
Deepening darkness.

Home

Good or bad,
it was never made
of bricks and stone:

once it was
apple trees and hedges,
sunlight on wet webs,

and long summer evenings
playing until the ball
could only be guessed;

or a place of cats,
content in the warmth
of my hope,

cuddled children,
read to and nurtured,
bathed and changed and fed;

slowly it became
a darkness where I hid
from resentments

under fathoms of frustration,
sunk into cold chasms
of loneliness.

Now I've woken
from sleep I've dreamt
all my life

to find,
with wonder,
home is your arms.

A White Rose (For Sophie Scholl)

In that dull land
of half-remembered
myths and glories

this is just
another emblem
on a beer glass,

the best pint
(and the cheapest)
in town.

But here they hold
this symbol close,
honouring a pure

young courage
that – loving life –
gave it,

hoping to wash
monstrous delusions
away with her blood.

Forest Walk

Birch cracks against bare birch
Whipped by the winter wind,
And strangling roots entwine,
Tightly binding a sudden
Turf-smooth clearing.

It's late, just time
To watch the ancient god
Complete a stately procession
Towards the clawing,
Bony fingers of the trees.

They criss-cross busily,
A complicated lacework etched
Into the darkening sky,
As the unforgiving shadow
Swallows the hope of dawn.

Kloster Andechs,
          Master Brewers since 1455

This beer has complex flavours.

Reformation, Enlightenment,
Wars and empires
Have come and gone

While the monks
Brewed their beer
And praised their Lord.

There's more than
Hops and barley
In this golden glass,

More than the softness
Of Bavarian water
Filtered through mountains.

You taste twenty generations
 Of pre-dawn rising
To contemplate the eternal,

Mixed liberally
With frustrated sexuality,
With yearning denied

Or only illicitly
Indulged, poured
Over guilt and grief,

And steeped
With high ideals
For centuries.

This beer has complex flavours.

Looking for Patterns in the Cafe Ruffini

Lovely
Munich cakes
and coffee
and tea,

Darjeeling
where my grandmother
(Rita-short-for-Margaret)
ruled my grandfather
while he ruled India

Loving
him and her five
boys and girls
she died
when they were

Small
children playing
on the nearby
swings and slides

Scream
in an ecstasy
of hurtling fear
kicking me where
I never want to go

Again
I sit
in the sun
staring nowhere

Close
when the
shimmering cobbles,
alive with ants,

Bring
me back:
the tea
was called
'Margaret's Hope'.

Oktoberfest on Election Day

Bavaria wears the sky as a flag,
White flecks woven with pale blue.
My daughter holds my hand
As we pass through the crowds,
Sometimes playfully slipping
My grasp, rehearsing.

In the tent a hairy leg
Stamps from bench to table
And through the fleshy frame
A woman gives me
A dark-eyed smile
Above her full bodice.

The waitress lends me a pen,
But I have to stand next to her,
Tethered by the attaching string.
She shows me her name,
Bettina etched on a brass broach
Pinned beside her breast.

Outside again the rain starts
With slow fat drops that coagulate
Into a hosing soaking deluge.
I hold the little girl in a tight embrace,
Pressed against the window
Of a ticket booth, protected

By a foot of overhang that keeps
The worst from her, but not
From the back of my cotton shirt.
Thunder cracks as lightning
Whips the Wies'n, and we cower,
Waiting for it to stop; waiting.

Later the long arms of fairground rides
Slip again into the evening; one way
The sky shades to white,
The other to an angry bar
Of Prussian blue. Flags hang
Limp in the dithering breeze.

I find my throat is sore:
I had tried to make myself heard
In a tent of raucous singing;
But now my croaking voice
Is too hoarse even
For bedtime stories.

Richard Strauss Fountain, Stachus

Water falls singing
In curtains of
Silver and diamond.

A young eagle
Circles high above
In pure blue sky.

People hurry past,
Alive in a poem
They won't read.

A New Year

The day fills up with snow
dragged by the ice-dawn's
half-light sledge
through the wreckage
of yesterday.

The cold, hard-edged city
silently loses
its straight lines
but finds sudden
 soft-plump freshness.

Tegernsee

Snow-etched mountains
melt themselves
into a pure lake,

just-liquid water
whispering to reeds
and stinging the shore.

Along the path
a little boy runs
further than he should;

a smaller girl chases
behind, ignoring
the winter wind.

On Flimsy Ground

The coral-filtered rock
Cooked slow in warm waters
Lapping on shores unknown
To the questing snouts of mammals.

Twisted contortions
Of precipice and crag still
Push relentlessly upwards
From that vanished sea floor,

Slashing the thin air
With razored edges,
And tearing the sky
With a dinosaur's jaw.

Südtirol, February 2018

Blasts of Cold Air

Frost flakes form
a mass migration,
butterflies
brilliant white on
the solid
surface of the lake.

Petrified,
a stilled cascade,
sculpted by
torrents of drying
wax from a
mountain of candles.

Sophie's Last Day

She knew she had
Only one thing to do
On that fine,
Sunny day:

Feel the surge
Of her young blood
Driven by her
Good, strong heart.

The Bomb

An infectious
Darkness climbs
To heaven.

The screaming stench,
Piss, burnt rubber,
Rubbish dump,

Mingles hopeless
Misery-fuelled
Blood-soaked dust

With poison drawn
To a lowering
Filth-stained sky.

A fungus grows
From the corpse
Of a horse.

Travelling with Philip Larkin

She thinks it might
Be hand luggage.
Smiling, I say
It's just a book,
But lose conviction:

It carries far more
Than it weighs;
Our eyes meet
Embarrassed,
And I climb aboard

To watch Europe drown
In a sea of cloud
Gently lapping against
The mountains
Like a premonition.

Travelling With e.e.cummings

i
-phones can't be
wholly a
-bandoned
(blinking in)
f-
light-safe mode.

i
-leave the book in-
(advertently)
on the air
(-o-)
plane

.

Departure

The tired old sun
Is hauled above the hills
To breathe vapid fire
 Into leaden clouds.

England's early birds
Sing of a coming spring
That lies far beyond
My sight and hope.

The Train to Dachau

Swifts weave in dogfights
With their projected shades,
Flitting between hop-poles
And crossing Maytime fields.

A dark background shadow
Defines a lasting scar,
A wound acknowledged,
Not allowed to fester or corrupt.

Here the poppies
And the cornflowers
Entwine with wild orchids
In the soft meadows.

The Train to Strasbourg

The frosty sunset
Burns a livid hole
In the crushed
Silk sky.

We travel backwards
Past fields and woods
Fought over
In pursuit of peace

By every generation
Before my own:
We just surrendered
Without a fight.

The Train to Nuremberg

Low yet intense,
the winter sun
burnishes the birches;

but the far side,
in deep shadow,
is etched in tarnished black.

The Train to Ingolstadt

Harvest-ripe slopes
Fold gently to a stream
And a village
Onion-domed church.

A flame-haired woman
Sits at the edge
Of a ploughed field
Beneath a blameless sky;

With her back to the world
She hugs her knees,
A basket laid beside her
On the rich earth.

The Ruins of Reculver

The Saxon chapel
and Norman church
built with stone
from the Roman fort
teeter on clay
cliffs undermined
by careless waves.

The tide still rises,
smacking the sea wall
and stranding wrack
high and drying,
green brown
purple pungent,
stinking of death.

Together

A cold wind
stirs the new leaves
to malicious gossip.

Cloud defined sky
is ruffled by
a blurring of wings

Insisting on train to Paris
their desperate
shared purpose.

Collecting

The sea spreads a flat calm,
white-warm as milk, and paler
than the ghost of polar ice.

With seaweed and feathers,
and the lament of the gulls,
each wave brings plastic;

The beach, and the cliff-top
town are painted by a man
with his back to the sea.

Broadstairs, 18.06.19

Streets that Lead to the Sea

I shall walk down
Streets that lead
To the Sea

Weaving between
Sullen old facades
gnawing the bones

Of their bitterness,
An unnoticed ghost
passing silent.

And on the beach
My feet shall leave
No footprints.

TGV - Munich to Paris Return

By the dark trees
Watch-towers stand,
Guarding the forest,
Preventing escapes.

One seems stranded
By the wood's retreat,
Alone, awaiting
The caress of spring.

At its feet, a sapling's
Branches whip old,
Bowed legs, bent
By weight, and decay.

The train speeds
Over the blood
And the bones
Of forgotten armies

As buzzards circle
Over plump-soft fields:
The landscape unfolds,
Like a drama.

Early Morning, Paris

the wail of the small child
accompanied by the drone
of a scolding hag
is an ancient song,

Belonging equally to
Syracuse or Thebes,
It's meaning
transcending language.

Boulevard Haussmann

Cast iron balconies
keep elegant facades
from the street

where sudden views
of Sacré-Cœur
open like memories.

Postcard from Budapest

The card he gave me
Was torn from a death
Stained notebook.

The language gives me
No reference points
(But the blood-clogged

Ear of a poet),
So I align myself
With the river;

We rattle up and down
While a genial man
Tells us Europe's too full.

For Miklos Radnoti

On a Toilet Wall in Budapest

I stand and deliver
Before ancient photographs
Of gorgeous women
In stages of undress.

Right before me dark eyes
Shine with a decadence
That felled the Habsburgs;
In this frozen instant

The warm full breasts
Draped in a tumbling shift
Promise a soft embrace,
And I fall a little in love.

I wonder if she succumbed
To Spanish 'flu or syphilis,
Or to something filthier,
Like war, or fascism.

I look at her forever
Lovely, forever young
And see how well
Her image became her.

Ireland

I. Exile

Driven onward
By foul winds
Through lands
Forever foreign;

A stranger,
Grasping at faint
Shades of smiles

To find somewhere
To sink dark-whitened
Roots into neutral earth
Claimed by others.

II. Kinsale

The day started bright,
But the clouds gather
Shadows of green

That glide across the fields,
Caressing spring-laden trees
And leaping the hedges
In their stride.

continues…

They ripple the water
Where the bay
Meets the open sea
And dance among

Gulls and hooded crows
On the wind
They brought with them.

III. Old Head of Kinsale
Rocks swallowed by boiling waves,
Bedding planes
Pointing skyward,
The stern of a sinking ship.

The crash of the surf
And the mournful
Cries of kittiwakes

Batter the cliff-top flowers
As sunshine cracks
On the black stone
And lies shattered on the water.

IV. Dublin
In the church
In Rathmines
In the beginning
Was the word;

A candle flickers
On each side of the aisle
Beneath a silent dome.

Philistine pilgrims troop
Round Trinity,
Jostling in beer-barreled rooms
Above the Book of Kells,

Deriding its purpose
And denying the honour
Due to scribes.

V. Ha'penny Bridge
The Liffey flows cleaner
As time sluices away
Shames and sins
Inflicted and imposed.

Around the corner
I can almost hear
The guns of my grandparents;

But the toll
For this bridge
Is a coin long-since spent.

Odyssey: Dublin Bay

Blackrock,
Dark stones,
Martello towers
Beneath round
Hills I feel I know.

Black rocks
I take
From the clear sea
Dry pale in
Unexpected sun.

Dublin:
The Green of St Stephen's Green

Every shade dances here,
In the trees marching
Towards the city,

In the grass lying thick,
in the hedges that hide
Lakes and statues,

In the undergrowth
Where birds rustle
With the restless

Ghosts of famine and Easter;
Every shade dances
On St Stephen's Green.

Photographs of Essen, 1930

Industrial background radiation
defines a timbered house
Soon to be consumed
by airborne fires;

An avenue runs through the snow
between the tsunamis,
to colliery spoil
and giant chimneys

Pointing to kinships behind wars,
towards railway arches spanning
a new objectivity
killed before the bombs fell.

To Albert Renger-Patzch

Trümmerberg, Olympiapark

Snow, not falling, driven hard,
A whirlwind caressing the steep slope
Built with the smashed remains of a million lives,
Collected and dumped at the edge of town.

A thickening coat of white now hides
The grass and the cobbles; but, angular,
Intrusive, the corner of a house brick protrudes
Through the soil and the winter.

Below, the swimmers and the skaters
Lap in trances of innocent concentration,
While the hill stands guard, a sentinel,
An eloquent witness, silently warning.

Being Driven to Austria

Lakes of mist collect
in bowls as offerings
to implacable gods

attended by the birches
blast-coated with ice,
and meringue-layered pines;

a shower of silver
draws a crushed-diamond
veil across the forest

just where the road
weaves between draped
frozen waterfalls.

Twist by twist
the turning road snags
the tattered remnants

of my englishness,
and the other small
things dragging behind.

Ramps

Waters spreading across valleys
From the Swale to the Danube
Bring out leaves, green in springtime,
Glossy in the glancing sunlight,

Plant and name as enduring
As its lingering scent,
Unchanged by the long-shipped
Descendants of Vikings.

In the woodlands of Europe,
United by folk-memory
And the subtle stink
Of wild garlic,

Language and peoples
Bleed together
In the shared worship
Of forgotten gods.

Common Ancestry

Black rock and white stone,
Washed up on shores
Of mingled distant tides,
Picked up and pocketed:

Chalk from spitfire-white-cliffs,
The crumbling buttress of delusions
That can be crushed wet
Between thumb and forefinger;

A dark particle of Romanticism,
Rosetta-stone-carved with myths,
Engraved by Yeats and defining
Space between Dublin and the sea.

I left the one to find the other,
Placing them side by side
To look at their balance,
And silently wonder.

A Different Sky

The charge that she felt
As their fingers touched
Was a light shining
Into the well-deep darkness
Of her grieving soul.

They might kiss,
Their entwined shadows
Cast by a sun setting
Into a limpid sea
They shall never know;

They might embrace
Under a different sky,
Beneath stars that fall glorious
From a clear night
They shall never see.

Waiting

A blackbird
pulls a worm
from the ground;

the worm
resists, and then
succumbs.

I feel the need
to try
or to try

not to try
to make
sense of it.

A gradual sun
parts the clouds
while the drying

wind shakes
rain drops
from the trees.

A Relic of Childhood

Seeing once more the
Old friend's stitched smile,
He remembers hugs
Tight enough to press

Part of a soul
Into a ragged heart
And make it skip
With a seemed beat.

The spell was
Omnipotent but mortal,
And in black bead eyes
He sees now only

The twice reflected failure
To love enough
And to ever
Be loved back.

We Are Making a New World
(After Paul Nash)

We all heard the bang
Of self-hatred
Exploding.

So much that was good
Will now be lost,
Sacrificed

At the altars of
Pot-bellied idols
Acolytes

Know to be false gods.
A darkness comes;
Hope dies last.

Gloucester, 7th July 2018

Look, stranger, on this island now…

Cowled seagulls lament
The ruins of Greyfriars
And its walled-in
Brutalism, decaying ugly;

In the pub a man
Tells impassive friends
Hitler gets a bad press,
And as I flee

A young boy swerves on a bike,
Drawing deeply on a cigarette
Dragged noisily into a bared chest
Browned by six-week sunshine;

At the bus stop, beside
Beggars rolling-their-own,
A drunk vomits between his feet,
And in the hot sticky night the gulls,

Mad with eternal man-lit day,
Ghost through dawn-hunted
Moonlight, and drift towards
Deep, dark seas.

Gloucester, 8th July 2018

The cathedral offers sanctuary
From the hot unenglish sun
Brazenly beating on the roof
And at the door;

I'm led up winding stone stairs,
Through ancient passageways
Hidden until revealed
By commonplace alchemy,

To the library, a hiding hole
For wizards, where monks
Guarded a treasury
Of bound-up words,

And where I hear
A Saxon scribe speaking clear
Through the cloistered protection
Of a thousand years.

His words collide in soft ripples
With the warnings of a mad
Soldier poet, and the choir
That first heard his voice.

PART TWO

A WOUND ACKNOWLEDGED

A Walk Through Berlin

Towards the Tiergarten,
Monsters of green iron
Cast for emperors
Define streets lining
Spaces stubbornly preserved
From the weight
Of concrete and history;

Cloaked in brown,
The hooded crows
Proclaim their difference
To English cousins
By reminding me
Of Ireland and Iraq.

The Broken Church's
Lopped-off spire
Punctures time, compelling
My eye to rebuild it,
My hand to sink
Into the sandy surface
Of a shrapnel-pitted wall,

continues...

And, beneath the empty
Rose window, a calculation:
Where to stand
To survive the blast-flung
Razor-stained-glass
Spray of death.

At Checkpoint Charlie
Students laugh in
Bright tourist sunshine,
Flashing their phones
And their smiles across
A shadow on the road
As they make friends & futures;

Where a grey division
Vomited overnight
A generation sinks
Into dotage, and forgets
Building walls
Is an act of violence.

September in the Park

Lamenting
gulls chase clouds
Across the sky

And a girl
Runs from swings
To metal slides;

The texture
Of the bench
Bleeds in my hand,

Beneath trees
Providing deep
Shade from the sun;

A brown leaf
falls, circling
slowly to ground.

Kaprun

Mist floods the valley
drowning white-coated
coral trees and the flat,
solid lake:

here cold tentacles
snatch ice crystals
from the air and sting
gloveless hands.

But as I climb I
strip away layers
to feel the sun's touch
on my neck;

sharp edged peaks reflect
an infinite
pure blue dome of glass
and diamond.

Snow-shod I stumble
upward, past skiers
carving tracks through the
man-made snow.

Cloud fills the valley,
an ice age's ghost
hiding the town with
ice-sheet fog,

obscuring the cars,
the industry
and homes with a new
veil of rain.

Kandinsky: Impression

Purple swirls and weaves
For all the saints
Dragged violently
From their humanity
Into iconic metaphor.

A forgotten boy sings a hymn
With all the gusto
The fine tune inspired
Amid the royal blues
And the woven bruises.

Lenbachhaus, Munich 14.9.18

Snow Shoes

Feet are placed
With oversized care,
Gaze confined to the path

Threading through trees
And fallen trunks
Temper-strewn by winter.

But now I'm surrounded
By soft-whipped whiteness
Smashed from diamond,

Pierced with dinosaurs' teeth,
Edges carved to a sky
Pure as a baby's eyes.

Dürnbach

Trees cloak
The mountains' shoulders,
Embracing me;

Fields roll green into blue,
Then gather grey
Where the peaks blend

With cloud and dissolve
Time into a past
And a future.

I shiver as shadow
Blows into the spring sky,
Bringing rain.

Schliersee

Each pine tree is meticulously painted
By Caspar David Friedrich.
They march up the flanks of the Wendelstein
All the way to heaven.

The mirror calm Schliersee is cold,
But not yet freezing.
The lakeshore branches dip into the water,
And delicate beards of icicles drape to
The steel blue, welding one element to another.

Hausham

The rain pours silver
From summits hidden
By a fallen sky

Advancing relentlessly
Through the breached
Defences of the valley.

Wisps of dancing-dragon
Cloud steam from the pines
Climbing the mountain ridge.

Passau and its Rivers

Nesting jackdaws collect twigs,
Silver necks and blue eyes
Gleaming in their gloss.

The Inn, mountain-clouded,
And the green-clear Danube
Flow together in milky separation

As Germany strains
At taut moorings
By the heart of Europe.

But a third river runs small,
Unnoticed through the gorge
It carved around the fortress.

Summit

The mountains
condense from the sky
as the cold sun
burns away the cloud.

Choughs, black-carved
into blinding brilliance,
hang on the thin wind,
joy-enduring.

My lengthening shadow
insists on the time,
and my expelled breath
freezes on my face.

Kronplatz, Südtirol

Nebelhorn (Oberstdorf)

The foggy mountain
Lives up to its name,
His flanks blanketed
In grey shrouds.

Below, a petrified
Stream steps headlong
In veils of molten wax
Forming cascading

Curtains of clouded glass,
Solid in the stillness.
But beneath, faint,
The stream rumbles.

DOK.Fest Press Conference

In the comfort
Of the darkness
I make notes,

Watching insights
Snatched for me,
Glimpses captured forever.

Snake-like I listen
With the strange
Tongue of my exile,

And my scribbled words
Overlap in patterns
I find hard to read.

Starnberger See

Birches are beaten
Into silver
By the sun,

But the water
Smashes the light
Into a million splinters,

While beyond,
Clouds collide
In growling darkness.

The View From Munich

Mountains range across
The southern horizon,
White and fused by ice
To the mint-cold sky.

There the wind roars:
On every knife-sharp ridge
A soul shouts unheard
Into the blasting storm.

Former Mining Village

Hollowed, it remembers
what it was for,
and what it cost.

Banks of cloud mass,
unanswered questions filling
gaps between steep slopes.

Snow falls on the mountain
but in the valley only rain.

Hausham, Oberbayern, January 2020

Alpine Forest, Nightfall

A shadow
Climbs the mountain
To cruelly tear the light

From the last
Desperate grasp
Of the dying sun.

A darkness
Bleeds into the valley
From an open wound,

And a bear's pelt
Lies draped around
The shoulders of a giant.

Love

Is a folk memory
Of a paradise
Most fear

Forever lost.
I am an Adam,
You an Eve,

With sticks
In our hands
To ward off snakes.

The Long Shadow

I can remember my grandfather,
An old man running
Then leaping over
A garden wheelbarrow;

But his father is as remote to me
As Alfred or Athelstan,
Just a name whose bones
Nourished an unknown tree.

They came from deep
Generations, rooted forever
In a place older than England;
Yet strange undirected currents

Carried them through
Glories and shames
To a mastery
Of a hundred peoples.

I cannot rest in this land betrayed:
Darker earth awaits me
Over an unquiet sea,
In the shadow of mountains.

Leaves

The floor is littered
with the yellow and gold
Of the downfallen summer;

They are the colours
Of an adventure
Made up as we go along.

My daughter and her mother
Discuss riding home
On the back of a bike;

I feel the disaster's loom,
See the blood,
Hear the screams,

But stay silent,
Fearing above all
To raise a timid girl.

As I walk home
Alone, a hedgehog
Rustles past, into a bush.

In the End

A tunnel
Collapses

Trapping the
Darkness

Letting in
Nothing.

Menorca

I found refuge
In a field of flowers.
Basking in the mid-day
A sow between litters

Lay giant, snoring
Soft in the corner.
And beside her,
A pile of stones

Marked the grave
Of an unlettered people.
Round my foot,
A snake lies coiled.

Time

The days go,
Accelerating
With the weight
Of accumulation

To line up behind
In a solid mass,
Immoveable
In the universe,

Forever familiar
Made utterly strange
By the tyranny
Of the eternal now.

The Sun Sails

The sun sails
Flawless in a
Deep blue sea
Towards a slow

Gathering of translucent
Cloud, darkening
To a dusk,
Bringing rain.

Young women
Ride past on bicycles
Smiling to themselves,
Remembering.

The End of April

Meadow flowers
Bow their heads
To the full moon;

A small girl plays
In defiance
Of the shadow

As the darkness
Gathers them
From the grass.

X-Ray

The shadows within
Define my bones
In ways I find strange:

Yet I know the aches
Of these fossils
Grinding on one another,

And I see their future
Exposed to sun or soil;
This is as much me

As my smile –
A flash of light
In a darkness.

The Struggle

Blind creatures push through
An impassive frost
To pink-nosed spring;

Their eyes blink open
Amid the flowers
And they begin

The cold brutal fight
To live, for a while,
in the sunshine.

To a Twilight

Galleon clouds,
Driven by winds
From strange horizons,
Sail towards a band of fire.

The sun is setting
In the west,
And the glory fades
Into night.

Film

The imprinted shades
Of an instant's
Captured soul

Wound tightly
Into a metal
Cased desperation

To make the fleeting
Flickering moment
Illuminate eternity.

The Legacy

We're all alone
In this
Together:

How to prepare
Our children
For the forced march
To the camp;

How to prepare
Ourselves
For the single bullet
That pitches us

Face down into
The ditch
They made us dig
With bleeding hands.

Will my blood-
Stained coat
Preserve the ooze-
Corrupted notebook?

To Miklos Radnoti

PART THREE

TO THE ONE

To the One

To the one
Who climbs the hill
Outside the petty town
To watch the sunset;

To the one
Leaving the cruel
Spectacle when others
Crowd in a flock;

To the one
Who, in a forest
Of outstretched right arms,
Folds his instead;

You are not alone.
I am with you,
Whispering
This in your ear.

Great Britain

Forests once marched unopposed
Through bear-haunted fiefdoms
Stalked by boars, and wolves,
And darker things given no names:
Every oak tree had a god.

For grind-hard centuries
Of hot-coursed blood,
Fervent hearts sought
Something bigger than gore-
Soaked petty kingdoms.

They stand now betrayed,
Sacrificed on a cold altar of myth:
Lies told to passionate
Fools cast adrift on a small island
Beset by storms.

Another Oktoberfest

After the parade
an old man
chooses not to look
at cleavages

And pretty open faces,
but instead stares
intently as the police
remove barriers.

Nearby a small boy
wears lederhosen
blissfully confident
they'll fit him forever.

November 5th

The children built
a wooden cage
around an oak sapling;

It burned alive,
a blood sacrifice
to savage gods.

Mountain Walk

The stony path
tramps steeply
through lynx-haunted hills,

More at its ease
going up
than coming back down.

Prophetic wind
pulls the ghost
from every hard breath

Foretelling
the coming
of a cruel winter.

The Last Day

The waves crash ashore,
Wet shaggy dogs
Shaking themselves
To soak bystanders.

A man and child
Dig on the beach,
Soon waist deep
In their frenzy

Of flying sand
Scattered to build
A desperate tunnel
Of escape.

Bayerischer Wald

Slowly the year dies.
In the sunshine
In the mist
In the mountains

The path winds down
Through painful
Hips and knees,
Collapsing the horizon

As the sun shines
In the mist
In the mountains;
The year dies slowly.

Travellers

The day ends,
Slowly toiling
Uphill, towards

The gold sky
A tired old sun
Just abandoned.

The Beaten Track

The path
Wove through a forest
To a clearing
That offered no more clues.

Shadows
Dance with the ferns
And the crowding
Pines whisper to the breeze.

A Fable (Part II)

The descent was rough
and bruising;
there's no return that way.

Before me a boulder-strewn
plain stretches pathless;
death feeds the flies.

The sun sinks,
casting purple shadows
that deepen to black.

Love

cannot be contained
in time,
in the world;

it spills over,
spiralling joyously
through the universe,

sparking points of light
where brilliant pathways
collide and conjoin.

Rehearsal, Winter Morning

Comfortable,
we lie together
entangled warm.

Unstoppable
the clock winds down
and I leave

Enfolded in
the cold embrace
of darkness.

The Future

We kneel on the edge of the ditch
we were forced to dig,
looking down into it;

Waiting.

Like Virginia Woolf

Loaded down.

Stones are packed
into bulging pockets,
heavy with failure.

A final creation
a gasp that fills
lungs with a river.

Spring

Lavender waves gently
To a willow tree
Dipping slender fingers
In a deep pool;

Roses drop their petals
Onto soft lawns
And a million birds
Sing to the butterflies.

The dew glints there still
Glorious in the sunshine,
Forever brilliant bright,
Forever gone.

March

Spring lies green in the valley,
But on the high ridge
Snow melts sorbet-slow
And trees are strewn,
Barring the path:

Winter, first a wild child,
Then a grumpy old man
Running amok with a stick,
Tore them up by the roots
Or snapped them wantonly.

Footprints walk before me
Through curtains of needles,
And over trunk-hurdles,
Clinging to the hope
That others found the way.

Ruins

Stones tumbled
in sheep-cropped turf
gather shadow;

The sharp edges
of shattered walls
slowly blunted

by blood-soaked ages
And the relentless
breaking of men.

April

Mist steals the mountains
and heaven lies hidden.

But the winter fades
into dissolving trees.

Socrates in the Marketplace

Warmth rises through him
from the stones beneath his feet.

Herb-scented winds
meander seaward
above the squealing
chatter of the crowd;

He sees bright threads
woven into thick dull fabric.

State of Emergency

A riot of silence
Overthrows
The familiar;

Trees become
Laden artworks,
Strangeness

Lying thick
On a changed world.
Still, the snow falls.

Forgiveness

The trees
shake their pelts

To shed
thick-lying snow.

It falls
through sunlight,

A dazzle
of diamond shards,

The ghost
of yesterday's storm.

If I Were to Make a World

If I were to make a world,
it would be like this,
with trees of coral
standing bare against
the new year's sky,
and snow lying deep
around their feet.

The mountains, etched
with silver edges
and dark graphite gullies,
stand immense and implacable,
waiting for a new ice age
to grind them down
when the sun grows old.

Eagles circle in the rare
clear air and the moon
rises once again full,
as evening draws
its pure blue cloak
around the shoulders
of the dying day.

The Mountain

A last climb lies ahead
into high woods
where lynx hunt hares.

My load is not heavy,
for I need nothing here:
the fresh thin air thrills,

Exploding my lungs
and bursting my skull,
exposing everything.

Eagles swoop to carry
food to their hungry young
in cliff-edged nests.

The Return

The sun still shines,
spring wakes.
A gentle breeze stirs
fresh green leaves,

And the murmur
of friends and lovers
mingles with the songs
of birds;

But slowly, unnoticed
the shadow creeps
over the meadow
and its flowers,

And a cold darkness
gathers itself
to smother us
as we sleep.

The Friends of Rupert Brooke

Loyal to a land
Of quiet virtues
Killed by lusting
Ambition and pride
In forgotten shames.

There's no peace now
In soil made small
By smallness;
And in foreign fields
Flowers stir, embattled.

For Denis Murray

Nightfall, Tegernsee

Cruelly bowed,
never again
straight or strong,

Birches worship
implacable cold-
hearted gods.

Ghosts rise dark
from the water,
drowning the valley.

Through Europe

I. Strasbourg

'Is that the frontier?'
asks the Indian next to me
as we pass the prison
on the outskirts of town.

I only noticed the border
because it's the Rhine:
the food's Teutonic
but better cooked,

German with a French accent
(and its terrible lineage)
is accepted here
with smiles.

II. The Bridges of Bruges

Creased silk laps against
bricks worn soft
by peace and war.

A pigeon's corpse lies
on sole-polished cobbles,
posed perfectly

Around a mass
of blood-stained feathers
and a broken heart.

III. Canterbury

Past boarded-up stores
he pushed a barrow
to the war memorial,

Heavy with soldiers' tunics,
laden with pips
and vivid medal ribbons.

Nearby a tramp lies
in a doorway, oblivious
to the grubby trade

In dead men's glory,
and the hard-won
legacy betrayed.

A Dream of Now and Then

My little girl
Throws off her shadow
To dance down the road
With her bobbing bunches.

In a long, long line
I see herded children
Ripped from fathers,
Clinging to mothers

Starved and scared:
Irrepressible, one skips
To a kind of victory
That completes the defeat.

A Big Stiff Whiskey

A yearning,
A deep retreat
To a cave, waiting

Silently to die
Alone in darkness,
Or the rounding

Up for communal
Slaughter and bulldozed
Burial in a pit.

Every Parting (is a Little Death)

Mist, frozen
to the moon,
bathes the darkness
in a pale light.

Sharp silver,
the cloud's edge
catches the sun
and hurls the dawn

Down mountains,
scattering
diamonds among
blue-green pine trees;

The valley's
black shadow
endures, its cold
surface iced hard.

Some Notes...

Shepherd's Warning
written on 17th January 2017, after Theresa May made one of her "major speeches" outlining her "plans" for Brexit.

Pippingford Park
A beautiful area in Sussex in Ashdown Forest, the model for The Hundred Acre Wood in the Winnie-the-Pooh stories. I wrote the poem while training conflict jounalists there.

Dinckley
Dinckley is a very small village in the Ribble Valley in Lancashire, close to Blackburn, the small town where I grew up.

Beyond is the Sea
Inspired by a beautiful photograph taken by a former colleague of mine, BBC cameraman Martin Roberts.

The Seagulls' Mourning Cries
Written on the centenary of the Battle of Passchendaele (Third battle of Ypres). My grandfather, Captain H. E. Howse MBE, commanded a company of the South Lancashire Regiment in the battle. They sustained heavy casualties. I wrote this poem after laying twelve roses on the War Memorial in Broadstairs, Kent. It was a gift from me, and my German daughter, to the men my grandfather led on that day, 31st July 1917.

Freesias By Her Bed
Freesias were the favourite flower of my mother, and the last thing she smelt as she died.

Wörthsee

A lake close to Munich, popular with bathers in the summer.

A White Rose (for Sophie Scholl)

The White Roses referred to are (in England) the logo of the Samuel Smith Brewery, and in Munich the name of an anti-Nazi group that peacefully resisted the Nazis during the Second World War. One of its leading figures was Sophie Scholl, who was beheaded for distributing anti-Nazi leaflets in 1943. There's a memorial to her in Ludwig Maximillian University in Munich. See also *Sophie's Last Day*, below.

Richard Strauss Fountain, Stachus

A fountain commemorating the Bavarian composer Richard Strauss in the centre of Munich. I really did see an eagle high in the sky directly above.

Kloster Andechs – Master Brewers since 1455

A monastery in the countryside west of Munich.

Oktoberfest on Election Day

Germany went to the polls on the 24th September 2017. I was enjoying the Oktoberfest in Munich, but got caught in a torrential downpour. I was also worrying about how many votes the fascist AfD would get.

Tegernsee

A mountain-rimmed lake in Oberbayern, south of Munich.

On Flimsy Ground

Written in Südtirol, the German-speaking part of Italy. It was part of the Austro-Hungarian Empire, then came under Italian rule after the First World War.

Sophie's Last Day

See *A White Rose* (for Sophie Scholl), above. Sophie Scholl went calmly to her death with the words "Such a fine, sunny day, and I have to go, but what does my death matter, if through us, thousands of people are awakened and stirred to action?"

The Train to Dachau

Dachau is a suburb of Munich, notorious for the Concentration Camp that operated there between 1933 and 1945.

The Train to Nuremberg

The city of Nuremberg in northern Bavaria was the location of huge Nazi demonstrations before the Second World War, and gave its name to the discriminatory antisemitic laws passed by the Nazis. It was also the venue for the trials at the end of the war that saw many leading Nazis condemned and executed for crimes against humanity.

Postcard from Budapest

Miklós Radnóti (1909-1944) was a Hungarian poet who was killed during a forced march at the end of World War Two. He was buried in a mass grave, but exumed, at the insistence of his widow after the end of the war. In his coat pocket they found a notebook which included his final works; these four "Postcards" are some of the finest poems written about the Holocaust. See also *The Legacy,* below.

Ireland

The old Head of Kinsale is the nearest point of land to the place where the *Lusitania* was torpedoed and sunk in 1915. It's now home to a memorial commemorating the 1198 people who were drowned.

My grandparents were married in the Church of Mary

Immaculate Refuge of Sinners in Rathmines in 1921. It was close to the main British barracks in Dublin (now the Cathal Bruga Barracks). My grandfather was a British officer, his new wife an Irishwoman whose two brothers were in the IRA.

The Book of Kells is an ancient manuscript kept in the library of Trinity College. Thousands of tourists troop past it every day.

Dublin: The Green of St Stephen's Green
St Stephen's Green is a beautiful park in central Dublin. It's also a mass grave of victims of the Great Famine of the 1840s, and was the scene of fierce fighting during the 1916 Easter Uprising.

Photographs of Essen, 1930
Inspired by the photographs of Albert Renger-Patzch (1897-1966), who recorded the industrial landscapes of the Rhur between the two world wars.

Trümmerberg, Olympiapark
A Trümmerberg is a 'rubble mountain'. Most German cities have them – built up with all the smashed remains of buildings destroyed in the Second World War. Munich's is in the Olympiapark, where the 1972 Olympics were held.

Ramps
Wild garlic is found all over Europe. Its norse name – *hram* – gave rise to Ramsgreave, the small part of Blackburn where I grew up, and also to Ramsgate, a town at the other end of England, close to where I lived in 2016. Wild garlic has a very distinctive smell and taste, and with my family I picked a large amount of it on the banks of the River Danube in Bavaria.

Common Ancestry
On becoming an Irish citizen after more than half a century as a Briton.

We Are Making a New World
(after Paul Nash)
Paul Nash (1889-1946) was an English surrealist painter known for his landscapes, including depictions of First World War battlefields.

Gloucester, 7th July 2018
The quote is from W. H. Auden

A Walk Through Berlin
Crows come in two varieties – one all black (native to England and many other parts of Europe including Bavaria), the other with grey-brown backs, known as Hooded Crows. The latter are found in Ireland, Scotland, Scandinavia, through northern Germany (including Berlin) and down into the Middle East.

The Kaiser Wilhelm Memorial Church was badly damaged in Second World War bombing raids, and has been left in its partially ruined condition as a memorial and reminder. Checkpoint Charlie was one of the main crossings between East and West Berlin during the Cold War.

Kandinsky: Impression
Wassily Kandinsky (1866-1944) was an artist who, in collaboration with Franz Marc (1880-1916) formed Der Blau Reiter – an expressionist art movement based around Munich and active before the First World War. He classified his work as Impressions ("direct sensations, received from outward nature"); Improvisations (visual representations of "inward nature", imagination and visions); and Compositions

(considered fusions of imagination, intuition and rational concepts).

Dürnbach

A small village in Oberbayern, close to the Tegernsee, and the site of a Commonwealth War Graves Commission cemetery.

Schliersee

A lake in Oberbayern. Caspar David Friedrich was a German Romantic painter who specialised in wild and desolate landscapes.

Hausham

A former mining village in Oberbayern, close to Schliersee and Tegernsee (see above). Being a mining village, before the rise of Hitler it was a socialist/communist voting area. In 1945 the Nazis fought the advancing Americans there – they chose the location partly because they wanted the village to be destroyed as an act of revenge for its earlier resistance to Hitler.

Passau and its Rivers

Passau stands on the confluence of two major rivers – the Danube and the Inn, and a third also joins there – the Ilz. There are several memorials to the victims of National Socialism in the town, but several leading citizens were influential Nazis in the Hitler era, and the AfD got 12.4% of second votes in the district in the 2017 federal election.

Nebelhorn (Oberstdorf)

Nebelhorn, in the Allgau district of Bavaria, can be translated as "Foggy Mountain"

The Legacy

To Miklós Radnóti. See *Postcard from Budapest,* above.

Bayerischer Wald

Bayerischer Wald is a wild area of hilly forest on the border of Germany with the Czech Republic. It is home to a great variety of wildlife, including European lynx which are currently being reintroduced to the area.

The Friends of Rupert Brooke

I worked with Denis Murray in Belfast in 2000, and was struck by a remark he made to the effect that so many British traitors have been public schoolboys. He was thinking of Philby, Blunt, etc, but it got me thinking about the self-sacrifice and responsibility displayed by previous generations – one clearly not shared by more recent generations.

I then discovered the Australian composer F. S. Kelly's *In Memoriam to Rupert Brooke* – Kelly was at Brooke's funeral in 1915, along with Bernard Freyberg (who I wrote about in my previous book of poems *Shadow Cast by Mountains).* Brooke was on his way to Gallipoli when he died from an infected insect bite; Kelly was killed later in the war; Freyburg, badly wounded and awarded the VC in the First World War, went on to be a general in the Second World War, and died in old age when his First World War wounds haemorrhaged.

A Fable (Part II)

See my poem *A Fable* in *Shadow Cast by Mountains.*

Patrick Howse grew up in Lancashire and worked as a journalist for 30 years.

He covered conflicts in Northern Ireland and the Middle East, and between 2004 and 2009 was bureau chief for the BBC in Baghdad.

He now lives in Germany, where he has found joy, inspiration and sanctuary among the people and landscapes of Bavaria.

Patrick holds dual UK and Irish citizenship.

Inge Schlaile was born in Munich, and studied Japanese at the city's Ludwig Maximillian University, before completing a masters degree in Organisational Psychology at London's Tavistock Centre.

She paints under the name Schlinge and has exhibited her work in California, London, Germany and Japan.